CARVER
POLICY GOVERNANCE®
GUIDE

Implementing
POLICY
GOVERNANCE
and
STAYING
ON TRACK

Revised and Updated

JOHN CARVER
MIRIAM CARVER

JOSSEY-BASS
A Wiley Imprint
www.josseybass.com

Published by Jossey-Bass
A Wiley Imprint
989 Market Street, San Francisco, CA 94103-1741   www.josseybass.com

Library of Congress Cataloging-in-Publication Data

Carver, John.
  Implementing policy governance and staying on track: a Carver policy governance guide / John Carver and Miriam Carver. —Rev. and updated ed.
    p. cm. —(The Carver policy governance guide series)
  ISBN 978-0-470-39258-4 (alk. paper)
  1. Boards of directors. 2. Corporate governance. 3. Directors of corporations. I. Carver, Miriam Mayhew. II. Title.
  HD2745.C37228 2009
  658.4'22—dc22

                                                                                    2009003152

Printed in the United States of America
REVISED AND UPDATED EDITION
HB Printing   SKY10077864_061924

"This makes sense! Let's do it!"

More often than not, board members exposed to a full description of Policy Governance respond by saying that they want to apply the principles and change the way their boards govern. It is gratifying when this happens, but what should the next steps be? What does it take to make the transition from habitual practices to thoughtful principles, particularly when those principles, although rational, are sometimes surprisingly different from what boards are used to?

We don't want to unduly restrain boards from implementing change, and we have no desire to sound discouraging, but it would be misleading for us to suggest that changing governance systems is a piece of cake. While it is possible to move to Policy Governance quickly (in as few as two to three months), making the change with inadequate learning and preparation can cause disappointment. Inadequately used, Policy Governance cannot live up to its potential of providing boards a path to effective and accountable leadership.

This is why we feel strongly about the most useful ways of implementing Policy Governance and why in this Guide we address the preparation for the change, the change itself, and steps for maintaining the change. We will look at policy writing, agenda preparation, policy manual maintenance, bylaw provisions, board member characteristics, and other real-life issues of governing. Before beginning, here is a brief overview of the model to remind you of its key features.

Policy Governance in a Nutshell

- The board exists to act as the informed voice and agent of the owners, whether they are owners in a legal or moral sense. All owners are stakeholders but not all stakeholders are owners, only those whose position in relation to an organization is equivalent to the position of shareholders in a for-profit corporation.

- The board is accountable to owners that the organization is successful. As such, it is not advisory to staff but an active link in the chain of command. All authority in the staff organization and in components of the board flows from the board.

- The authority of the board is held and used as a body. The board speaks with one voice in that instructions are expressed by the board as a whole. Individual board members have no authority to instruct staff.

- The board defines in writing its expectations about the intended effects to be produced, the intended recipients of those effects, and the intended worth (cost-benefit or priority) of the effects. These are *Ends policies*. All decisions made about effects, recipients, and worth are *ends* decisions. All decisions about issues that do not fit the definition of ends are *means* decisions. Hence in Policy Governance, means are simply not ends.

- The board defines in writing the job results, practices, delegation style, and discipline that make up its own job. These are board means decisions, categorized as *Governance Process policies* and *Board-Management Delegation policies*.

- The board defines in writing its expectations about the means of the operational organization. However, rather than prescribing board-chosen means—which would enable the CEO to escape accountability for attaining ends—these policies define limits on operational means, thereby placing boundaries on the authority granted to the CEO. In effect, the board describes those means that would be unacceptable even if they were to work. These are *Executive Limitations policies*.

- The board decides its policies in each category first at the broadest, most inclusive level. It further defines each policy in descending levels of detail until reaching the level of detail at which it is willing to accept any reasonable interpretation by the applicable delegatee of its words thus far. Ends, Executive Limitations, Governance Process, and Board-Management Delegation policies are exhaustive in that they establish control over the entire organization, both board and staff. They replace, at the board level, more traditional documents such as mission statements, strategic plans, and budgets.

- The identification of any delegatee must be unambiguous as to authority and responsibility. No subparts of the board, such as committees or officers, can be given jobs that interfere with, duplicate, or obscure the job given to the CEO.

- More detailed decisions about ends and operational means are delegated to the CEO if there is one. If there is no CEO, the board must delegate to two or more delegatees, avoiding overlapping expectations or causing disclarity about the authority of the various managers. In the case of board means, delegation is to the CGO unless part of the delegation is explicitly directed elsewhere, for example, to a committee. The delegatee has the right to use any reasonable interpretation of the applicable board policies.

- The board must monitor organizational performance against previously stated Ends policies and Executive Limitations policies. Monitoring is only for the purpose of discovering if the organization achieved a reasonable interpretation of these board policies. The board must therefore judge the CEO's interpretation, rationale for its reasonableness, and the data demonstrating the accomplishment of the interpretation. The ongoing monitoring of the board's Ends and Executive Limitations policies constitutes the CEO's performance evaluation.

Step-by-Step to Implementation

Given this review of the Policy Governance model, more completely described in the Carver Policy Governance Guide titled *The Policy Governance Model and the Role of the Board Member*, let us now turn to the process by which a board can transition to the use of Policy Governance and maintain its new governance excellence. We begin by looking at a sequence of five steps we've found most workable for implementation.

Step One: Initial Learning—What's New and What's Over

Amazingly, we find that some boards are anxious to omit this stage. They argue that a couple of their members went to a Policy Governance workshop or that a few board members have read some or all of a book on Policy Governance and that therefore the board should proceed directly to the policy-writing stage. We feel so strongly that it is wrong to leap into a change as great as that to Policy Governance without full understanding, that as consultants we will not accept business from such boards. Policy Governance is so different from what boards generally do and requires so much group discipline that to undertake its use before fully understanding it is unwise. We are not arguing that board members must be as expert as Policy Governance consultants, but that they should have at least enough understanding to be able to explain to an interested observer why the board governs as it does and why the principles of Policy Governance are too important to cut corners. Attempting to apply principles you are unaware of or even unsure of guarantees that results will be less than they could be.

Board members and even CEOs who learn about Policy Governance often want their boards to be introduced to this powerful model. It is very useful for the board to find a way to learn the principles together as a group, and it is quite acceptable for any board member or the CEO to initiate this process. We recommend, however, that while it is fine for a CEO to suggest that the board may find the model useful and arrange a seminar or provide written materials, the CEO should not lead the process after that stage. If the CEO leads, there is a strong risk that the board will not take ownership of the process, diminishing the opportunity to exercise active leadership about its own job.

> So if you are a board member, adopting Policy Governance is one of those situations where starting the machine before reading the instruction manual is not a good idea.

For boards that can afford qualified help, learning Policy Governance should minimally entail a daylong seminar offered by a trained consultant. Consultants without sufficient training in the model's theory and practice often make grave errors in trying to teach it. Just as examples, if you are working with a consultant who tells you that the board decides ends and the staff decides means or that the board can't speak to the staff or that it can't use committees or that your strategic plan is your Ends policy, his or her understanding of the model is simply wrong. If your board cannot afford qualified help, carefully reading the materials published on Policy Governance is a must. It is less foolproof than obtaining live help but much better than nothing. If cost is a factor, it might work to share training workshops with other boards in your community.

If your board is highly visible, such as a school board, city council, or chamber of commerce board, it is important at this early stage to involve those publics that frequently observe and critique it. Citizens, media, trade association members, and unions are all examples of groups that can be quite vigilant about what their board is doing. If these observing groups do not understand Policy Governance, they could become concerned and even obstructive about the board's process, since it will not look like what they expect. If these groups have the same opportunity as the board to learn the model, the risk of misunderstanding can be minimized. Our emphasis here is not so much how these groups relate to the ownership, but their importance in making the board's transition to Policy Governance easier or more difficult, a more or less political consideration.

If yours is the board of an organization that is heavily regulated, such as a credit union, insurance company, or city government, including your attorney in the learning is a wise decision. Your attorney will be able to assist the board in determining what steps must be taken (usually on a Required Approvals agenda) to ensure that regulated aspects of the organization are in legal compliance. Likewise, involving a representative of the regulator is not only wise but courteous; the board can show this important figure that the rules will be followed, albeit by a different method.

An important part of the learning that must take place is developing an understanding of which time-honored and maybe even well-loved practices a board would have to stop if it uses Policy Governance. Examples are the approval of staff documents, board members using individual authority, and boards spending large amounts of time receiving reports about what has gone on inside the organization.

Equally important, of course, is a board's learning what it must do that currently it rarely, if ever, does. The board must learn that its job is real, not ceremonial, and has outputs to produce. It must learn that it has to be in charge of its own job, a task that requires a great deal of group discipline. It must learn that it will spend time separating ends from means as well as large issues from smaller ones, speaking with one voice, focusing on the future, and judging only against prestated criteria.

It is not uncommon to find that these changes are unattractive to some board members. They may have joined the board precisely to do what is now not to be done. Their commitment is real, but if the board decides to adopt Policy Governance, they must adapt or resign and be expected to do so by their colleagues. Starting out a new system with people avowed to resist it is counterproductive. In any event, the responsible question for board members to answer is "Is this a tool that will allow us to govern more accountably on behalf of the owners?" rather than "Does this suit my own needs or does it conform to activities that have become familiar and comfortable?"

So if you are an experienced board member, your greatest strength with a new paradigm is your willingness to learn and try out new behaviors, not your years of experience. Your experience of what has worked and not worked in your other board service may be more hindrance than help.

Often at the conclusion of the initial learning stage, boards are able to decide whether or not to use the model. Some boards, however, are still undecided at that early point. We occasionally hear that a board is interested but yet unsure about whether the model would be a governance improvement worth the effort or uncertain what using it would be like. Board members tell us, "We understand the principles, but they are abstract. What would it look like for us?"

Whether boards know they wish to proceed to the implementation of Policy Governance or whether they think they might wish to proceed but are unsure, we recommend the same next step.

Step Two: Writing Means Policies—Means Before Ends

Step two in our five-stage sequence is writing policies. The full use of Policy Governance requires that the board has created its policies in the four policy categories, but you can begin initial use of Policy Governance if only the Means policies have been developed. By Means policies, we mean operational means and governance means, the latter divided normally into Governance Process policies and Board-Management Delegation policies. Board policies about operational means are called Executive Limitations because they place boundaries on CEO authority rather than prescribing organizational methods and actions. You may need to refer to *The Policy Governance Model and the Role of the Board Member* to fully refresh your memory about these categories.

The idea of starting with Means policies often comes as a surprise. You may be wondering why we don't recommend starting with ends. This is a good question, for there would be nothing technically wrong with starting with Ends policies. But we don't generally recommend it, for Ends policies are difficult and slow. Often boards believe that the ends of their organization are self-evident, but they rarely are, requiring a good deal of study and thought. (We will capitalize *Ends* when referring to a board's actual Ends policy documents but use lowercase when referring to the idea or concept of ends.) The value choices to be made are challenging and, in addition, they are long-term in nature. It is very hard for board members to be as intently future-focused as writing Ends policies requires if they are worried about what is happening in the present and if they are unsure of how their group process should proceed. Determining ends is somewhat easier if the board has already settled issues of its own process and if it has already instituted the new way of controlling the ongoing decisions and practices of its staff.

Writing the Means policies is a lot easier than writing Ends policies. All Policy Governance boards describe their rules for themselves (Governance Process) quite similarly, and if they use a CEO function, they describe their manner of delegation to the CEO (Board-Management Delegation) very similarly too. In fact, these two policy areas are the board's own personal statements of Policy Governance principles. Likewise, policies are similar among Policy Governance boards in the Executive Limitations area. This may be surprising to you, but let us remind you that the Policy

> So if you are a board member, keep in mind these new policies are like a concentrated laundry product. They pack a huge amount of meaning into a few words.

Governance board does not make policies about the means that the CEO should use, which would differ greatly from one organization to another, but about the means that the CEO is not authorized to use. Because these policies are founded in a board's values of prudence and ethics, the fact that we are all different in many respects does not eclipse our similarity about prudence and ethics.

Because the policies in the three means quadrants are quite similar among Policy Governance boards, it is possible for boards to write them from a sample starter set. These policy samples have been published in several books and are helpful in guiding the thinking of boards when they describe their own values in these areas. It is, as we all know, much easier to use a sample than to start with a blank sheet of paper. It is also much more economical than asking every board to reinvent the wheel. The most recent set of these samples are in *Reinventing Your Board* for nonprofits and governmental boards and, for equity companies, in *Corporate Boards That Create Value*.

So if you are a board member with experience on other boards, do not compare this policy writing to previous experience.

We suggest you use our samples when doing your Means policy work because they are entirely Policy Governance consistent. Using the policies developed by another board exposes you to the risk that you will be working from documents not fully Policy Governance–consistent. We strongly recommend that your board use a trained Policy Governance consultant, for even with the use of samples, policies can be tailored in a way that reduces the utility of the model. Having qualified help allows you to minimize the risk of mistakes and avoid wasting time.

The board should draft its Means policies as if it has decided to use the model, even if it hasn't. Approaching the task with this mentality will ensure a more thorough job and one that avoids rewriting if the decision is made later to go ahead with adopting the model. Also, in writing the policies, it is necessary to define policies strictly using the "any reasonable interpretation" rule, not assumptions you might be tempted to make about your current CEO's or CGO's likely interpretations. Board policies are not to be written for specific incumbents of a position but for the position itself, since they reflect board values about issues, not second guesses about others' decisions.

Writing Means policies is best undertaken in a workshop setting with the entire board. Board members who cannot show up should be expected to respect the work of those who do. Otherwise the same work must be done and redone. Using trained help, you should be able to complete the Means policy writing in two to three days. It would be nice to say that it could be done in two to three hours, but this is not the case. Remember you are making decisions that will allow your board to control its entire organization through its written values. If you do not use trained help, we are unsure how long the process will take. Trying to do the policy writing a little at a time in board meetings will likely cause the board to lose both its momentum and its focus on the principles of the model.

Your CEO is an immensely useful resource. He or she has a great deal of information that will be useful during policymaking, so to exclude the CEO from the workshop would be a waste. Have the CEO there and expect that he or she will include staff members who can be helpful. But let nothing obscure the fact that the process is board work, not staff work. You and your colleagues are making governance decisions; asking the CEO to make the decisions rather than merely to have input into them displaces your work onto him or her.

> So if you are a CEO, your role in board meetings is not to see that the board does a good job, though you do have knowledge the board can use. See yourself as source, not savior.

If your board governs an organization that is highly externally regulated and you accept our suggestion that you include your attorney and a representative of the regulator, you must be sure all understand their roles. They are not present to make your decisions for you but rather to see that their legitimate interest in lawful compliance is included in your work. Both must be Policy Governance knowledgeable. If they do not know Policy Governance, they will not be able to be as helpful or as reassured as if they do.

Step Three: Tidying Up Your Work— "What Did We Overlook?"

The board at this stage has made major progress toward being ready to implement Policy Governance if it still chooses to do so. It will have moved ahead with preparations while maintaining its prerogative to terminate the process. At this point, we recommend that the board pause and institute a review of its work. Having followed the Policy Governance rules carefully, it is unlikely that there are significant gaps in the work the board has done, with the planned exception that the board has yet to write Ends policies.

It is prudent nonetheless to check to see if any previous board decisions that are still in force, though not formulated as Policy Governance policies, contain board values that should have been transferred into Policy Governance policies. Examples may include a previously crafted investment policy or energy conservation policy. Simply inserting them as they are into the set of new Policy Governance policies will cause inconsistency in the emerging system, weakening the use of the model. Therefore, the board must consider whether aspects of those previous decisions add usefully to the new set of draft policies, then be sure any useful features are transferred into Executive Limitations policy language and format.

Another kind of further check is essential for particular kinds of organizations. Highly regulated organizations are often required by government or funder that the board itself make certain decisions rather than delegating them. Public school boards in the United States and Canada, for example, are required to approve teacher hiring, even though everyone knows that this is handled by management. Policy Governance boards deal with these requirements by having such decisions placed on the Required Approvals agenda.

This special agenda within the normal agenda is used this way. The board is informed by the CEO that he or she has made decisions that an external authority requires the board to ratify. Along with that information, the CEO should provide monitoring evidence that the matters were handled in a manner consistent with applicable board policy. As a result, there is no reason for the board not to approve or ratify the decisions, since disapproval constitutes renunciation of the delegation. Approval can be swift and lawful. Boards may need to ask their legal counsel to assist them to identify which decisions delegated to the CEO need board ratification. In this way, the attorney can isolate the issues that should be found on the board's Required Approvals agenda.

We have often described the Required Approvals agenda as a variant of the more commonly known consent agenda. But the only similarity is that each can be passed by the board without discussion and in a group. They are very different in how and why items come to be on this agenda within the agenda. For example, being routine or noncontroversial are not reasons for putting items on this special agenda. The only reason is that an outside authority demands board action on a decision the board has delegated to the CEO. Further, because board action will have given decision authority to the CEO, a single board member cannot pull an item from this agenda unless he or she is alleging that board policy was not followed as the CEO made the decision. To pull an item from the Required Approvals agenda for any other reason would be to "undelegate" the authority to make the decision.

> So if you are a board member, listen to any points your CEO wishes to share about this momentous decision, but be certain you cast your vote according to your best judgment as to what will be in the best interests of the ownership, not of the CEO nor even of the board.

The attorney may also be helpful in identifying if and how the board has made policies that are in conflict with the bylaws of the organization. This is useful as it identifies the parts of the bylaws that should be amended. We will discuss bylaws issues later in this Guide.

At this point, the board is in a position to decide if it will proceed with the implementation of Policy Governance. This is a board decision, unrelated to the preferences of the CEO or staff. The board does not govern in the interest of its CEO; rather it governs on behalf of the owners.

If a board finds that it is not willing to proceed with implementation, it can govern as it had been governing in the past. Up to this point in our five-step process, nothing official has been changed. Learning Policy Governance followed by writing and checking the Means policies have only set the stage for change. But if the board decides to proceed with Policy Governance implementation, it now takes step four.

Step Four: Setting the Date—Jumping the Canyon in One Leap

Following the board's decision to implement the Policy Governance model, and given that it has its written Means policies in place, its next step is to set the implementation date. Because moving to Policy Governance involves a system change, it is important to remember that systems are changed only after the new system is carefully constructed. Incremental improvements to an existing system can be phased in as desired, but this is not how you move from one system to another. Accordingly, we recommend that the board set an implementation date and establish it with a motion passed in a board meeting.

The motion should state that as of a certain date, all board documents (this does not include bylaws) are repealed, to be replaced by the Governance Process, Board-Management Delegation, and Executive Limitations policies just written, signaling that the board has undertaken the use of the Policy Governance model. The documents repealed tend to be resolutions, policies, budgets, and other plans. Board members upset about the loss of these documents might feel better knowing that the documents do not disappear but become documents of the CEO and open, of course, to CEO alteration.

Setting a date to make a system change is not as scary as may first appear if we remember that the board can spend as much time as it needs in preparation. But when it's time to make the change, the new system cannot safely be phased in, any more than a nation's driving on the left can be changed to driving on the right in stages.

You will notice that the new system is implemented without Ends policies. This is not a situation that should continue for long; after all, the ends of your organization describe the reasons for its existence. But with Policy Governance implemented, the board has the time and focus to attend to its all-important ends decisions. The matters that had routinely been on its agenda are largely delegated to the CEO, so the board's job now looks very different indeed. If you are nervous that your board will be proceeding without Ends policies, it may help to reflect that it didn't have Ends policies before either and that when the board uses Policy Governance, ends deliberation becomes its major focus.

Step Five: Preparing the New Agendas— Where Do We Go from Here?

Before arrival of the implementation date named in the board's motion, we suggest your board spend time preparing its agendas for the next few meetings. We advise planning board agendas at least a year in advance. It is important to have agenda plans ready when the board holds its first Policy Governance meetings. Boards that have not planned for the new kind of agenda can feel intimidated or disoriented by the change to the Policy Governance model. It is not uncommon to hear board members wondering what they will be doing after implementation. We even hear the mistaken supposition that there will not be much to do. A good agenda plan changes that.

So if you are a board member who voted in the minority against moving to Policy Governance, you have an important duty: your duty is to observe the new rules even if you dissent. Your alternative option is to leave the board.

The first meetings under the board's new Policy Governance need not be intimidating or anxiety-provoking. Along with the agenda plan the board makes, the CGO's fine tuning and implementation of it should cause a transition that is fully anticipated and understood by the whole board. Having made a successful transition to Policy Governance, the board faces its continuing governance responsibilities armed with new tools. Let's now turn, then, to board agendas as they begin and continue in perpetuity.

The Board's Agenda—not the CEO's Agenda for the Board

We made the point in the Carver Policy Governance Guide titled *The Policy Governance Model and the Role of the Board Member* that boards should be in charge of their own agendas, rather than relying on their employee, the CEO, to tell them what to talk about. We emphasized that the board's job is largely not a real-time job but a future-focused job.

We do not mean that the board must do its work with no assistance whatsoever. Certainly the logistics of board operations can be handled by staff. Examples of such logistics are the compilation and distribution of material, the provision of meeting space and amenities, the maintenance of documents and Web site, travel arrangements, and so forth. As long as administrative support is, in fact, really *support* and not the *content* of governance decision making, there is no problem. In Policy Governance, this is normally accomplished in an Executive Limitations policy that prohibits the circumstance in which the board has insufficient logistical and clerical assistance. The CEO, on whom all Executive Limitations are imposed, may fulfill the requirement by making adequate staff assignments.

When the board makes a plan for its work, it starts by looking at its job description. Policy Governance boards use job descriptions that describe the outputs of their job rather than the processes they use to accomplish the job. Based on the board link between owners and operators, the need for clarification of values that will guide the organization, and the board's accountability for operational success, Policy Governance boards describe their job outputs, at minimum, as

1. connection with owners,

2. written governing policies, and

3. assured organizational performance.

Item 3 is equivalent to a manager's job output of "subordinates' success" advocated by some management theorists. It simply means that a person's or group's accountability for the work of subordinates is not fulfilled if those subordinates do not produce what they should. Put another way, unless the CEO is successful, the board cannot be.

Some boards have additional items in their values-added job description, outputs that they could have delegated to the CEO but chose not to. Responsibility for donor funding is one; legislative change is another. In both cases, these or other job outputs of a board beyond the irreducible minimum are determined by the circumstances of a given organization. They are not generic to all boards, and so they are not part of the generic Policy Governance board job description. Items that appear on the board's job description are not delegated to the CEO, so the board must take direct responsibility for their accomplishment.

So if you are a board member, voting to add an optional output to the generic board job description means you and your colleagues are really going to produce that output. It does not mean that the staff is going to do it with board assistance, that the board is going to do it with significant staff assistance, or that the staff is going to do it but bring it to the board for approval.

Although the Governance Process policy that describes these outputs is often titled "Board Job Description," it could also have been titled "Overall Board Agenda." The board engages in activities, including meetings, in order to do *its* job (as opposed to someone else's job), and this policy describes its job. Keep in mind that the job description to which we refer is a list of outputs, not a list of activities. So it is an enumeration of specific organizational characteristics (for example, that there exists a meaningful link between owners and operators) for which the board and the board alone is responsible. We ask boards to be suspicious if they can't relate items on their agenda to some part of their job description; they should suspect that they may inadvertently be doing part of the CEO's job. If they are, they are compromising their ability to hold the CEO accountable.

As you can see, this job description does not describe what the board will be doing at, say, the April meeting. It does not do so because the overall job description is a broad, inclusive policy: like all policies, it begins at the widest level. Further defining the elements of the board's job allows the board to identify its various components. Let us look at what a given board might further define.

Sequential Levels in Defining Board Job Outputs

The job output "connection with owners" might be further defined as

   a. A clearly defined ownership

   b. A clear identification of diverse subgroups within the ownership

   c. A clearly articulated set of questions on which owner input is desired

   d. A plan for meetings with or surveys of elements of ownership to collect answers to these questions

The job output "written governing policies" might be further defined as

   a. Board decisions that create new policies or amend existing policies

   b. A policy manual that is up-to-date, complete, and used by all board members

   c. Ends policies written in two levels of detail by (date)

The job output "assured organizational performance" might be further defined as

a. CEO hired (date) (for boards that need to hire or replace a CEO)

b. Monitoring system operational by (date)

c. Decisions regarding CEO remuneration by April 1 of each year

d. Auditor under contract to the board by March each year

e. Timely action taken in the event of evidence of consistent unacceptable performance

The further definitions of the board's job products shown above are examples of what a board may decide its focus over the next year or two should be. They are more detailed than the policy as it was initially defined but still do not describe what the board will do at its April meeting.

If it chooses to do so, the board can go into even more detailed definition of its work, planning a six-month agenda. But if the board can accept any reasonable interpretation by the CGO of its agenda policy as it stands, it would leave the fine details of the meeting-by-meeting agendas to the CGO and expect that its work over the year would amount to a reasonable interpretation of what it committed to accomplishing in its job description and other applicable policies. It is in this way that a board can be in charge of its own agenda, one with a primary focus on ownership linkage, value clarification (most significantly, long-term Ends policy formulation), and certainty of performance.

In other Governance Process policies, the board will probably have signaled its commitment to the maintenance of its own skills through education and self-evaluation. It may have committed itself to the finding and orientation of new members and the accumulation of certain decision information. These commitments also find their way to the board agenda by way of the CGO's reasonable interpretation of all the board's policies in the Governance Process and Board-Management Delegation categories.

A Board Meeting Agenda

So what does a Policy Governance board's agenda look like? Because we cannot know what any particular board might have included in its agenda plan, we cannot say for sure. Policy Governance agendas vary from board to board and for a given board from one time to another about as much as do those of non–Policy Governance boards. But we do know that Policy Governance boards spend little time listening to reports of staff and committee activities. They tend to have few items on the agenda, but those items are of great import. These relatively few decisions are of very high leverage, and because of the explicit, ongoing policy-based focus, these decisions are almost always couched as amendments to existing policies or the creation of new ones.

Here is a sample board agenda, presented with the caveat that it is not a prescription but an illustration.

Sample Board Meeting Agenda

1. Call to order [Important to establish that the meeting is valid.]

2. Attendance [Important as a part of group discipline and to establish a quorum—absentees who have failed to meet the attendance requirement should be noted and action taken.]

3. Minutes of last meeting [Important to verify that the areas of focus and all decisions made by the board at its last meeting are accurately recorded—we discourage verbatim minutes because since individual voices carry no authority, they are unnecessary.]

4. Monitoring Reports received since last meeting [As evidence of due care, the board must judge whether monitoring reports demonstrate the accomplishment of a reasonable interpretation of the policies monitored.]

5. Major agenda item according to agenda plan [This item and the next are expected to take the most time and yield the most substantive deliberation.]

6. Major item according to agenda plan

7. Proposed amendment to Executive Limitations Policy 4.2, changing wording from "xxxx" to "yyyy"

8. Self-evaluation or rehearsal exercise

9. Adjournment

Item 7 is an example in which one or more board members ask the board to consider a policy change. It is good practice to ask board members who are not satisfied with a board policy to suggest an amendment and to identify the information that would assist the board in making the decision.

Other than items 5, 6, and 7, most agenda items should not take long to complete. Monitoring reports, which always compare CEO interpretations to board policies, then data to CEO interpretations, are extremely important but not normally time-consuming. Board members should receive the reports in advance in order to be able to arrive at the meeting having already read them. The judgment of the board should be straightforward and decided in the same way that the board decides anything else, for example, by discussion followed by a vote. You will find more about monitoring reports in the Carver Policy Governance Guide titled *Evaluating CEO and Board Performance*.

We strongly recommend, as shown on the sample agenda, that a board check its own performance through self-evaluation at every meeting. We also advise that the board frequently perform skill-building exercises like solving rehearsal scenarios. We discussed self-evaluation in the Guide titled *Evaluating CEO and Board Performance*, so here let us expand briefly on rehearsal exercises.

Individual proficiency at a task requires practice. That is true for musicians, athletes, and marksmen. But if it is true for individuals, it is even more strikingly true for groups. Consequently, practice for symphonies, sports teams, and infantry units is essential—in fact, so essential that practice requires far more time than performance itself. Governance is a team effort, yet despite its crucial role in the work of society, practice is virtually unheard of. Policy Governance brings to boards a system of leadership, one that like all systems calls for meticulous use of a tool. The tool itself is important, to be sure, but its adept use is just as important.

The Policy Governance model equips a board with a carefully crafted tool, capable of guiding competent and dedicated people through all the challenges of governance. Most boards most of the time are not confronted with life-or-death tests of their competence; after all, most day-to-day life is, well, day-to-day. But missteps by the board when such a challenge does arise can have grave consequences. Practice for boards involves the board presenting itself with a real or imagined scenario and using its policy manual to establish, first, what has already been said about the matter; second, whether the decisions to be made in the scenario are the board's to make; and third, whether its existing policies are adequate. The purpose of regularly scheduled rehearsals is to maintain governance skills and in effect to make the governance system work. The former benefit is obvious; the latter comes about because any weaknesses in the policy system are uncovered and corrected long before they become problematic.

> So if you are a board member, be thoroughly conversant with the relatively small number of policies Policy Governance causes the board to have. You can use them either to resolve or to point to the resolution of any governance problem that arises.

We are unable to say whether Policy Governance board meetings are typically longer or shorter, more or less frequent, or more or less satisfying to board members. Certainly, for boards that spend long hours in meetings into the wee hours, Policy Governance meetings may be considerably shorter. But boards that skim over their work in short lunch meetings may find serious deliberations cannot be accomplished that way. Meeting frequency is a variable each board should decide for itself to fit the task as it develops, unless, as is the case for some boards, meeting frequency is controlled by governmental or accreditation authorities. (With Policy Governance in mind, it is easy to see their requirement as a damaging prescription of means.) Whether board meetings are more satisfying depends on what board members like doing. Those who love the big picture, wrestling with difficult choices about the future, operating from 30,000 feet, and empowering others will love the process. Those whose interests go to budget lines, purchasing procedures, and programmatic involvement may decide board work isn't fun anymore. But the test of a governance approach is not whether today's board members enjoy it but whether tomorrow's owners are represented by an informed and authoritative board.

Maintaining the Policy Manual

It is unusual for the total of board policies in Policy Governance to require more than thirty pages. This brevity results in a slim policy manual that contains all policies in the categories Ends, Executive Limitations, Governance Process, and Board-Management Delegation. If your policy manual has hundreds of pages, you are unlikely to know what is in it. You really have no excuse for not knowing what's in thirty pages. In addition, the policy manual's utility is that it contains all of what a given board has said that is still in force. But this is only true if the manual is kept up-to-date.

Most decisions made by Policy Governance boards are to amend a policy or add a new one. These new or amended policies should be transferred to the manual, which is most manageable if in looseleaf or electronic format. Since it is hard to imagine how a Policy Governance board could get through a meeting without referring to its policies, it is important that everyone on the board have a copy that is complete and up-to-date. The accountability of the board secretary is that board documents are complete and up-to-date, and this therefore becomes the most important part of the secretary's job. If the secretary is a board member, the board should allow this officer to use a small amount of staff time, as the logistical issues are usually dealt with by staff. But the accountability to the board is the secretary's.

Group Discipline: One for All and All for One

Frequent, policy-based self-evaluation and rehearsals can help the board gain and maintain expertise in the use of Policy Governance due, of course, to recurrent checking and practicing. But there is a mind-set also crucial to maintaining an agreed upon discipline as a group: the mind-set is that of taking responsibility not only for your own participation and action but also for the success of the group. This is a subtle but powerful distinction. It is easy to wait for the chair or some other board member to intervene if the board goes off course, but true group responsibility would demand that every member of the group accept the obligation to intervene if the board is not doing its job. So it is that being responsible for one's own behavior is insufficient for group discipline to flourish; one must also be one's brother's keeper.

So if you are a CGO, the tricky job of demanding the board observe the discipline it has committed to in Governance Process and Board-Management Delegation policies falls to you. The board needs neither milquetoast nor manipulator but greatly needs a compassionate disciplinarian bound by the board's own words.

You may have noticed that it is apparently easier to call attention to unhelpful board behavior in the hallway or parking lot than in the boardroom. But it is only by calling attention to it in the boardroom that anything useful can be learned and errors corrected. Without that, one vociferous and insistent board member can stall the proceedings of the entire board, in effect holding the board hostage without the assistance of firearms. When this happens, don't blame the insistent board member; rather blame everyone else, for other than momentary interruption, the offending member cannot offend without the tacit acquiescence of other members. A situation like this—quite common in boards everywhere—illustrates that the other members, happy that they are not behaving irresponsibly, are actually failing in their duty to group responsibility.

> So if you are a board member, be wary of unanimous votes. They may mean board members are squelching their dissent or the issues voted on are not important enough to dissent about.

Failing to master the group responsibility challenge is to surrender governance to the interpersonal impediments in group process. We hope it is clear that we are not prescribing hostile confrontations. We are calling upon board members to learn approaches for reminding each other of the rules to which all are committed, thus moving past stalemates. Having subjected those rules to group decision making to begin with and having committed them to often-reviewed policies, the task is easier.

The board should acknowledge that its job is to decide issues about which people disagree. It should expect disagreements and develop an atmosphere in which debate is encouraged. Indeed, it should seek as much relevant input from as many diverse sources as it can, thereby intentionally increasing the disagreement. Trying to avoid disagreements—rather than embracing them with a sturdy, practiced foundation of group discipline—thus handicaps knowledgeable performance of the board's job. Honor diversity, but don't get paralyzed by it.

> So if you are a board member, you have every right—even an obligation—to voice your dissent with other members but not to impede the process of deliberating and deciding.

With open input along with respectful and vigorous debate, it should be possible for board members, even those who voted against a motion that passed, to agree to support the legitimacy of the board's decision. There is no need to pretend to agree with your board's decisions if you really disagree, but it is improper to undermine a legitimate decision legitimately arrived at. As to board members continuing in a public way to express their dissent, Policy Governance does not limit this right, though individual boards may choose to do so.

Recruitment and Orientation: Filling Positions, Not Warming Seats

No one would find it acceptable for an operational organization to focus more on filling positions than on filling them with the properly trained or experienced applicants. Having all the positions filled is not in itself a virtue. Yet boards often feel so compelling a pressure to let no seat go vacant that they are loath to be as careful in filling vacancies as staff are. The board's job as owner-representative is a crucial one, making it mandatory that great care be taken finding board members.

So if you are a CEO, you must treat any board decision, no matter how split the vote was, as if it were unanimous. Moreover, the board's Ends and Executive Limitations policies are not a menu. You cannot pick and choose ones you think important enough to attend to or that fit your vision.

Just as board agendas logically flow from the job products or values added expected from the governance role, so should the characteristics to be sought in new board members as well as expected in existing ones. The needs for each board will differ, of course, due to widely different circumstances of different industries, types of organization, environment, and jurisdiction. The boards of an international relief organization, large petroleum company, local health center, and professional society differ in ways that defy generalization. But in other ways, they are all the same. They each are groups with accountability to a legitimacy base (members, shareholders, community) for the proper conduct of enterprise. To use the Policy Governance model requires some generic skills and attributes.

Characteristics to be sought in board members include:

- Knowledge of, commitment to, and closeness to the ownership

- Comfort with the diversity within that ownership, with its competing opinions and values

- Commitment to inclusive and fair process

- Comfort with accepting responsibility and the shared authority it imposes

- Respect for the authority of others

- Acceptance of a role that carries no individual authority

- A focus on the big picture and the future that is visionary yet practical

- Ability to participate assertively in group process

- Ability to accept and not undermine a group decision legitimately made

- Time available to participate fully in preparation and in actual board work

- Capacity for conceptual flexibility and for addressing high-level issues in a disciplined, careful process

- Ability to uphold group rules and to follow those rules with respect to relationships with staff and others

- Willingness to play a role in making judgments about the performance of the CEO, but only in relation to preexisting criteria

Our list is not complete, as we continue to find more skills helpful to being a responsible board member. Some of what we omit, however, is intentional. For example, we do not include skills that would be helpful to staff, for the board exists to be the owners' voice, not to help staff. (Individuals may help staff if asked, of course.) We do not include fundraising or lobbying abilities unless a board has chosen to hold itself responsible for donor funding or legislative change.

Even with new board members chosen perfectly, however, proper orientation is vital, particularly since their understanding of Policy Governance may be minimal. We recommend orientation for new members prior to their being officially seated. Let us emphasize that the training we mean is in the board's adopted governance process rather than in the jobs of staff. The familiar orientation to organizational details is not in itself harmful but can easily detract from new members learning that their job is not to understand management but to practice governance.

Bylaws: Basic, Not Boring

We noted earlier in this Guide that we would make a few comments about bylaws since your board will probably be reviewing them as it transitions to Policy Governance.

Bylaws may be controlled by the board or they may be controlled by a more authoritative body outside (though perhaps including) the board. It is common, for example, for association memberships to retain control over bylaws. In either event, the purpose of bylaws is to describe how the artificial person created by the government's granting of incorporation can assume reality by being tied to real humans. Bylaws are positioned in a hierarchy of documents between the governmentally granted corporate charter and subsequent corporate decisions that in Policy Governance would be the board's policies. These board policies precede and control all decisions at the executive levels.

In their bridging function from corporate charter to board decisions, bylaws make clear that if an assemblage of real humans is in specified ways chosen, given notice, and presented an issue, a favorable response by a certain number or percentage constitutes a valid decision by the artificial person, that is, by the corporation. In other words, bylaws give the artificial person the ability to decide and to speak. Bylaws should describe who has standing as either a member of the corporation or as a voter in determining who is placed on the board, under what circumstances board members can be asked to leave the board, and what constitutes a valid board meeting and a valid board decision. In jurisdictions where certain forms and purposes qualify an organization for favorable tax treatment, there are other requirements bylaws also fulfill, particularly as related to the method by which disposal of assets will be carried out in the event of the dissolution of the corporation.

Since bylaws are harder, sometimes far harder, to change than policies, it is important not to place in the bylaws decisions that need not be there. A common example is the inclusion in bylaws of a list of board committees. Sometimes, as in an association, there is reason for the broad membership to create a committee for its own purposes (rather than for the board's purposes). An example could be a committee that organizes the nomination of board members. Such a committee should be listed in the bylaws because it belongs to the members. But committees intended to help the board in its job need not be mentioned in the bylaws. The board can decide for itself what committees it needs from time to time. There is no more reason for a membership to foist such a means on the board than for the board to foist means on the staff.

We look for the following bylaws items that could make the use of Policy Governance difficult or that could reduce the accountability of the CEO to the board.

Number of Board Members   The more board members there are, the harder it is to be a disciplined and task-centered group. Make the board as small as possible. Policy Governance does not address an exact number, for great variation is called for. But a useful rule is never to have more than seven without good justification. Larger boards are often advocated in order to be more representative, yet the most meticulously representative group (requiring many members to reflect the many differences among owners) will doubtless find itself unable be in charge of itself, falling victim to one or a few who take the reins, even with no ill intent. A board that cannot govern itself cannot properly govern an organization.

Attendance Requirements   We often read bylaws that state that board members who do not attend X of Y meetings without good reason may be asked to leave the board. You have probably noticed that on many boards, any absence is excused if the absentee is courteous enough to phone ahead, thereby allowing as many absences as that board member chooses. The permissive language in "may be asked to leave the board" is hard to enforce, since a motion that this or that board member be expelled is socially awkward. If the board has a real job to do, having board members show up to do it is important. Being too busy to serve on a board is understandable, but agreeing to serve on a board and repeatedly not showing up is irresponsible. We suggest bylaws language such as "Board members who do not attend X out of Y meetings will be deemed to have resigned."

Quorum   You are no doubt aware that many boards, particularly nonprofit boards, have a large number of members but a quorum requirement that can be as low as one-third. Even the more typical 50 percent plus 1 requirement is an open admission that attendance doesn't matter and can result in the group of people who make the decisions in February being a substantially different group from those who made the decisions in January. Certainly no one would tolerate staff attendance being treated in the same manner. We recommend a high quorum requirement. Should it be 100 percent? This is not probably realistic, but count down from 100 not up from 50 when finding your board's quorum requirement.

Officers   We look closely at bylaws language describing the role of the chair and treasurer. Frequently we find that the chair is described directly or indirectly as the CEO, perhaps unintentionally.

That can be done by saying the CEO is "supervised by the chair," that "the CEO reports to the board through the chair," or other language that puts the chair between the board and its CEO. This language should be changed unless it really is the board's intention that the chair should have all the authority and accountability of a CEO. Despite its prevalence in many businesses, the combining of chair and CEO in one person presents a clear conflict of interest. The treasurer position is often described as responsible for financial management, a role that conflicts with the job of the CEO. If your board is required to have a treasurer, the bylaws should describe the role as ensuring that the board is adequately knowledgeable to write sound Executive Limitations policies about financial issues. Other officer positions are less likely to interfere with delegation from the board to the CEO but should be changed if found to do so.

Committees   As we argued previously, unless the members of the corporation wish to have their own committee and prescribe it in the bylaws, committee prescriptions should be omitted. The board can decide in its policies if, from time to time, it needs one or more committees. We are particularly concerned about executive committees because they are often granted authority to, in effect, *be* the board between board meetings. Such a board-within-the-board sometimes becomes the board-over-the-board. The very existence of such a committee usually signals that the board is (or thinks it is) too large or otherwise unable to do its job.

Prescriptions of Operational Means Such as Programs or Services
These should clearly be removed. The Policy Governance board does not prescribe operational means, so bylaws that do so are out of order.

Conclusion

In this Guide, we have focused on the steps to be taken by your board to transition to the use of Policy Governance. We have also looked at documents, mind-sets, and practices that will help it stay on course. Your experience of board work will change drastically. The more mechanical aspects of board life will also change, such as committee work, length and frequency of meetings, certainly content of meetings, and interaction with the ownership displacing some of the previous interaction with staff and its activities.

The point, of course, is not the board experience but the degree to which the board fulfills its moral and sometimes legal obligation to the many people who do not and will not ever sit at your table. In this meaningful and difficult challenge and opportunity, we wish you and your board success in and enjoyment of the high calling of governance.

About the Authors

John Carver is internationally known as the creator of the breakthrough in board leadership called the Policy Governance model and is the best-selling author of *Boards That Make a Difference* (1990, 1997, 2006). He is co-editor (with his wife, Miriam Carver) of the bimonthly periodical *Board Leadership*, author of over 180 articles published in nine countries, and author or co-author of six books. For over thirty years, he has worked internationally with governing boards, his principal practice being in the United States and Canada. Dr. Carver is an editorial review board member of *Corporate Governance: An International Review*, adjunct professor in the University of Georgia Institute for Nonprofit Organizations, and formerly adjunct professor in York University's Schulich School of Business.

Miriam Carver is a Policy Governance author and consultant. She has authored or co-authored over forty articles on the Policy Governance model and co-authored three books, including *Reinventing Your Board* and *The Board Member's Playbook*. She has worked with the boards of nonprofit, corporate, governmental, and cooperative organizations on four continents. Ms. Carver is the co-editor of the bimonthly periodical *Board Leadership* and, with John Carver, trains consultants in the theory and implementation of Policy Governance in the Policy Governance Academy.

John Carver can be reached at P. O. Box 13007, Atlanta, Georgia 30324-0007. Phone 404-728-9444; email johncarver@carvergovernance.com.

Miriam Carver can be reached at P. O. Box 13849, Atlanta, Georgia 30324-0849. Phone 404-728-0091; email miriamcarver@carvergovernance.com.

Notes